For my family
and my friends
Olivier

The finest chateaux around Paris

TEXTS
Uwe Bennert

ILLUSTRATIONS
Olivier Audy

ENGLISH ADAPTATION
David W. Cox

PARIGRAMME
jeunesse

Just about everyone knows about the chateau in Versailles.
But who knows why it is so huge? Who can explain what the Hall of Mirrors is? And why is it that the sprawling grounds also have two other palaces, the Grand Trianon and the Petit Trianon? And what is the reason for two different types of gardens, the formal French garden style and the more natural landscape garden style? Lots of questions pop up when you visit this famous chateau.

Ile-de-France (the greater Paris area) has many palaces spanning periods from the Middle Ages to the 19th century. Some of them are not very well known, but they all represent the periods when they were built. Visiting them shows you the differences between a castle from the Middle Ages and a palace from the Renaissance period. What is a "*donjon*" (main tower)? What is a "pediment"? What do we mean by "Louis XIII style"? The answers to all these questions can be found by visiting the castles in La Roche-Guyon, Provins, Vincennes and Maisons-Laffitte.

French chateaux are not only loaded with fascinating architectural history, they are also chock-full of stories about the people who lived in them. From King Charles V to Emperor Napoleon III, by way of King François I, these buildings give us glimpses of major figures in French history like Anne de Montmorency, Diane de Poitiers, Nicolas Fouquet, King Louis XIV, Queen Marie Antoinette, and so many more.

Castle construction did not stop once the French Revolution had overthrown the monarchy. Palatial dream homes were built in the 19th century. People like the famous novelist Alexandre Dumas and the wealthy banker James de Rothschild had splendid homes built for them that were just as impressive as the great castles from the past.

Pierrefonds

COMPLETELY

REBUILT

Eight high towers stud this enormous fortress called Pierrefonds. At the end of the Middle Ages, a prince with a passion for art constructed this castle. Prince Louis, Duke of Orleans, was the brother of King Charles VI.

At the dawn of the 15th century, architects had to adapt their designs to accommodate integrating new technology: artillery! Firing canons made walls shake. The thick walls at Pierrefonds had to absorb the destructive vibrations. Two walkways, one right on top of the other, ran along the top of the walls. The lower walkway was positioned on brackets called machicolations. In an attack, these walkways gave defenders of the castle an advantageous firing point. At the turn of the 17th century, the castle was torn down on the order of Cardinal Richelieu (King Louis XIII's powerful minister). Its big towers were seen as a potential challenge to the king's power. For over two and a half centuries, Pierrefonds lay in ruins. Then, one day, Emperor Napoleon III decided to renovate it. He put Viollet-le-Duc, a famous architect, in charge of the project. Using lots of imagination, Viollet-le-Duc reinvented the castle's medieval architecture, sculptures, murals and furniture. All over the castle and inside its courtyard, there are sculptures of fanciful animals. Some of them are really pretty funny.

Versailles

Versailles started out as a basic, but royal, hunting lodge, built for hunting enthusiast King Louis XIII. In 1661, his son Louis XIV decided that the place needed improvements. The young king hired the most brilliant artists of the day to create the gigantic chateau that we know today. Why construct a palace so colossal with three levels and a seven-hundred-meter-long garden-side façade? Was it designed solely to house the royal family and their servants? Certainly not! The king had a vision and a plan. As the head of an absolute monarchy, Louis XIV made the nobles of France and their families come live in Versailles in order to control them. Roughly three thousand people resided in the chateau. This way, every day, each of them would notice that the king did indeed have absolute power. His motto, "I am the State!" ("L'état, c'est moi !") is famous still today. Also known as the "Sun King", Louis XIV gladly showed off his power. He was always the center of attention in his palace.

THE SUN KING'S IMPRESSIVE ESTATE

King Louis XIV

Louis XIV did more than construct palace buildings. He also ordered and coordinated the planning for the entire city of Versailles. He paid close attention to the design of his sprawling palace grounds with their pleasant canals, fountains and sculptures. Sumptuous outdoors parties were held there to celebrate his glory. Some lasted for days and included fireworks and jetting water. Whether viewed from the city or from the gardens, the chateau was the focus from any point of perspective. Numerous kings and princes across Europe admired and copied the example given by France's Sun King.

The Hall of Mirrors

MIRRORS, MIRRORS!

Enormous shimmering mirrors and crystal chandeliers sparkle in the vast Hall of Mirrors located in the center part of the palace. Big mirrors along the wall stand opposite the windows that open out onto the gardens. The sweeping view from the center window follows the perspective from the fountain basins, carries onwards over the Grand Canal, and out into the distant forest. This great hall was initially named the "*Grande Galerie*", which certainly stands to reason as it is no less than 73 meters (240 feet) long.

It was here that the king met with foreign ambassadors, held parties and royal weddings such as the one for Louis XVI and Marie Antoinette. The royal family would ceremoniously walk through the Hall of Mirrors to reach the palace chapel.
Louis XIV wanted to impress his guests. He ordered highly ornate decorations for this grandiose hall and particularly for the ceiling. Louis the Great, who was very proud of his military exploits, never missed an opportunity to recall his victories over his strongest neighbors: Germany, Spain and Holland. Le Brun, one of the chateau architects who was also a fine painter, executed large paintings glorifying the military victories of Louis XIV and France. But centuries have passed, and nowadays, we tend to associate the Hall of Mirrors with the Treaty of Versailles which was signed in this very room in 1919. It marked the end of World War I.

The Grand Trianon

FAR FROM THE COURT…

King Louis XIV began living in the chateau at Versailles with his family, the court and the government in 1682. He imposed a set of strict rules which became called "court etiquette".

The king's daily activities were set to a strict timetable. Privacy was out. Almost everything the king did was public. To start with, several hundred lords would be present each morning when he woke up. Next, he went to Mass, then he met with his ministers. After this, he was served lunch. Lunch was always followed by a stroll through the grounds. From 8:30 AM to 11:00 PM, the most powerful man in the kingdom rarely had a minute to himself!

It is easy to understand why the king would want to be alone or with his family from time to time. This is why he had a smaller palace built relatively close to the big palace. He bought up the lands of a small nearby village called Trianon, had it completely torn down, kept the name, then built a new chateau on the site. The difference between the Trianon and the main chateau is huge. Unlike the *grand chateau*, the buildings here are all ground level. The decoration is white and pink marble from quarries in the south of France. Still today, the interior decor is from the Sun King's period but the furniture is from the time of Napoleon I. He, too, enjoyed staying in this chateau from time to time.

Two courtiers

14

The Petit Trianon

MARIE ANTOINETTE'S DREAM WORLD

Queen Marie Antoinette

A different period in time, different customs. King Louis XV was not the son but the great-grand-son of Louis XIV. The generation gap as huge. The young man thought the Grand Trianon was too formal. Therefore, he had the Petit Trianon built further away. The four high columns on the façade made it look like an ancient Greek temple.

The interior was cosier than either the sweeping halls of Versailles or the big rooms in the Grand Trianon. King Louis XVI, the grandson of Louis XV, gave this smaller chateau as a present to his wife, Marie Antoinette. The queen never much liked the constraints of court life. She found this place not only quieter but more in keeping with the styles of her time. Tastes had changed since the reign of Louis XIV and the queen did not really approve of the formal (or French-style) gardens that the Sun King had commissioned from Le Nôtre. From Marie Antoinette's point of view, the straight pathways, the straight rows of trees and the shaped bushes were a far cry from Nature. She thought that mankind should not prune plants and trees into artificial shapes. The garden she chose for the Petit Trianon was picturesque. Everything was planted to give the impression it had sprung up naturally. The French call this an "English-style" garden.

The queen lived in an ideal little world here, which she found very much to her liking. In the end, she became blind to the misery of the people. In July 1789, the French Revolution caught up with her and she was never allowed to return to her Petit Trianon hideaway. She and her children left Versailles several months later and never returned.

VERSAILLES

Malmaison

THE IMPRESS'S COUNTRY HOME

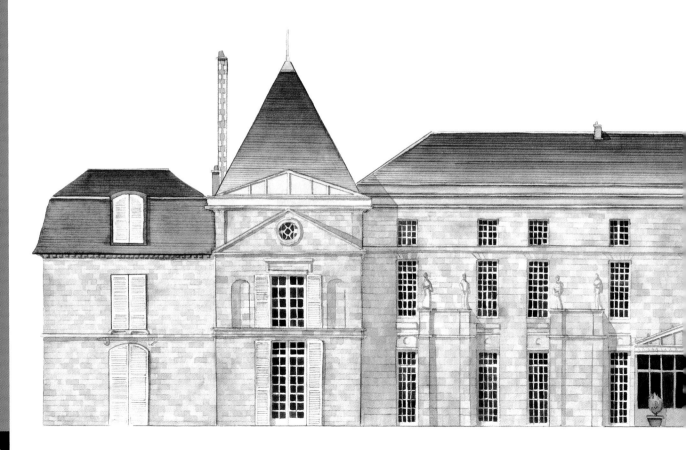

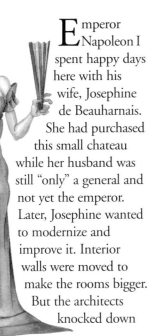

Empress Josephine

Emperor Napoleon I spent happy days here with his wife, Josephine de Beauharnais. She had purchased this small chateau while her husband was still "only" a general and not yet the emperor. Later, Josephine wanted to modernize and improve it. Interior walls were moved to make the rooms bigger. But the architects knocked down too many walls and the building started showing signs of strain. Before it collapsed, they consolidated it with hefty pillars. These buttresses were topped with statues recuperated from the park of the Marly Chateau, which had been one of Louis XIV's favorite residences.

An up-to-date chateau requires up-to-date furniture. At that time, ancient art (Egyptian, Roman and Greek) was very much in vogue. After all, Napoleon's goal was to make France as powerful a nation as the Roman Empire, but with him as the emperor. A new style was born! "Empire" was its name. It is particularly recognizable inside the chateau: the *vestibule* (in other words the entrance) is decorated with marble columns and busts that top pedestals just like in ancient Rome. Elsewhere, mural paintings, chandeliers and the rest of the furnishings evoke antiquity. Malmaison has at least two fun oddities. Napoleon was a great warrior. And so, his council room at Malmaison was fitted out to look like a huge military camp tent. Josephine loved tropical plants. As she was from the island of Martinique in the tropical French West Indies, the palace was set up with a pretty garden where she could grow amazing exotic plants that she had imported from all over the world.

La Roche-Guyon

IMPREGNABLE

A cliff-hanger! This medieval castle literally hangs from a white cliff and overlooks the village below and the Seine River. Curiously, the oldest parts of the castle (early 12th century) are actually the highest up. Actually, to be perfectly precise, the very first castle was dug into the rock and was a series of interconnecting grottos. Therefore, that big medieval watchtower that we see today was the second stage in the fortress's development. This donjon tower served the defenders of the castle as a last refuge when the enemy had invaded the rest of the fortress. But it was also, first and foremost, the symbol of the local lord's power.

An impressive set of double walls surrounded the donjon in order to defend the lord's dominion. Originally, the donjon was four stories high. Soldiers on the top floor could survey the countryside and river to keep an eye out for approaching enemies.

This donjon was terribly uncomfortable. That is why a fortified castle was built further down the slope. A secret passage connects it to the donjon.

The buildings that we see today underwent major modifications over the centuries. The outer walls were torn down and windows were widened to sizes that would have been impossible to defend back in the Middle Ages.

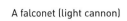

A falconet (light cannon)

Fontainebleau

HOME OF KING FRANÇOIS I

Right from the Middle Ages, French kings like Philippe Auguste and Louis IX (also known as "Saint Louis") loved staying at Fontainebleau. But it was in the 16th century that King François I made this castle his preferred residence. Like most kings, he enjoyed hunting and, naturally, greatly enjoyed the vast forest nearby, which still today attracts enthusiastic visitors.

The old medieval castle, however, was not at all to the king's liking. He decided to renovate it along the lines of the stylish new palaces he had seen in Italy during his military campaigns there. This decision marks the beginning of the Renaissance in France. The word "renaissance" means re-birth or bringing to life concepts and techniques from Greek and Roman antiquity. The king brought in top Italian artists to decorate an enormous hall within his castle. It is called the "*Galerie François Ier*". The frescos (wall paintings) illustrate the king's major achievements. The painting technique used was unknown in France at that time. The artists were not painting on wood or on canvas but directly onto the fresh plaster that was still moist.

King François I invited one of the greatest artists of the Renaissance to live in France: Leonardo da Vinci. His famous portrait of a noble Italian lady with a mysterious smile draws crowds from the world over to the Louvre museum in Paris. This painting was originally part of the Fontainebleau castle's art collection. The name of the painting? *Mona Lisa* in English and *La Joconde* in French.

King François I

Sceaux

Colbert was a powerful and rich minister under King Louis XIV. He bought a small chateau then enlarged it. The construction began at the same time as the construction of the king's opulent residence in Versailles. But very little remains of Colbert's chateau. There is only the main entrance and the twin guardhouses used to keep a watch on the door. Why was the rest demolished? Because it belonged to aristocrats and during the French Revolution, privileges of the nobility were being abolished. The chateau was sold, neglected, fell to ruin and eventually had to be knocked down. The chateau we see today did not go up until the last half of the

19th century, during the reign of Emperor Napoleon III.
Inside, you will find the Museum of Ile-de-France. Its collections include paintings, ceramics and other items that tell the history of Ile-de-France (the greater Paris area). Just left of the main entrance is another Colbert-period building that houses temporary art exhibitions. This building was the chateau's former orangery. Orange trees and fragile plants from warmer climates spent the winter in this building. In summer, these potted trees and plants were rolled out into the park to make it more attractive. The beautiful grounds offered vistas and pruned trees similar to those at Versailles. But then, this is hardly surprising as a certain Mr Le Nôtre was in charge of landscaping both palaces.

Minister Colbert

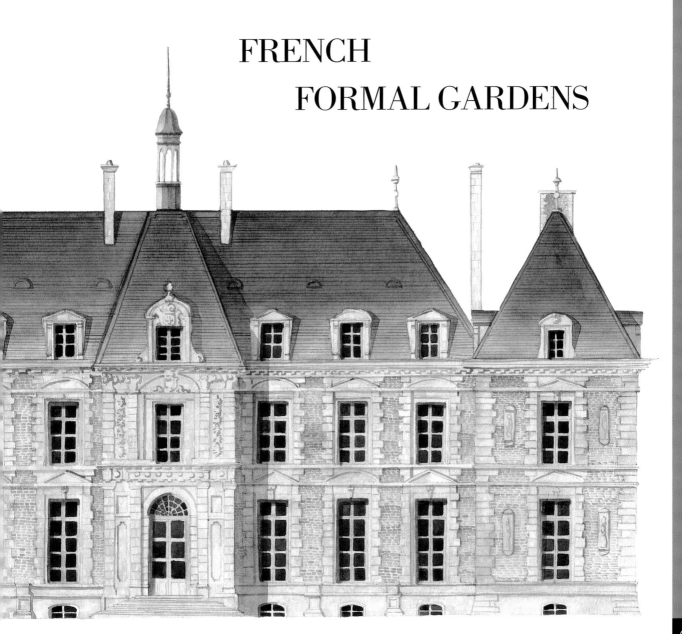

FRENCH
FORMAL GARDENS

Monte-Cristo

A MUSKETEER'S DELIGHT

This was the home of famous writer Alexandre Dumas. No mere house, he built a veritable palace! Dumas' famous book *The Three Musketeers* made him rich enough to afford his dream home. Upon a close look at the façades, we notice that they imitate the Renaissance. Above the main doorway are two imaginary birds holding a medallion, which contains the portrait of the owner of the house. Obviously, the man was very proud of his home.

Like most writers, he needed peace and quiet. Dumas built a garden-office. His novels' titles were engraved on the outside walls of this building. Dumas jokingly referred to it as his "*Chateau d'If*", an allusion to the prison of one of the characters of his most famous novel: "The Count of Monte Cristo". And Monte Cristo was the name he gave to his own home.

Like the Count of Monte Cristo, Dumas became rich, had everything he had ever wanted and enjoyed opening his doors to guests. The motto engraved on one wall reads, "I love those who love me." That was sufficient invitation for parasites who came knocking at his door. Dumas not only let them stay but held big parties to entertain them. As a result, just four years later, Alexandre Dumas had accumulated massive debts and had to sell his palatial home for a pittance. It had cost him a fortune. Only one room has kept its original interior decoration. This is a first-floor drawing room fitted out like an Oriental palace.

Writer Alexandre Dumas

Vaux-le-Vicomte

A MINISTER'S DREAM

The motto beside the squirrel on Nicolas Fouquet's coat of arms reads, "How high won't he rise?" ("*Jusqu'où ne montera-t-il pas?*") This man was very sure of himself and convinced of his power. But, he had every reason to be because he was the Minister of Finance under King Louis XIV.
A man that important needed a home that showed his high rank. Fouquet hired eighteen thousand workers to tear down three villages for the space he needed. Once his magnificent castle and its grounds were completed, he held a big party and he invited the King and the Court. Fouquet spared no expense. Only the finest would do to impress his guests. He hired Vatel, the most famous cook of the time, to prepare a luxurious dinner. Molière and his troop of actors put on a play. Dazzling sprays of water spurted from the

Minister Fouquet

fountains. Fireworks lit up the night sky. Fouquet was thrilled. Little did he know how much danger he had put himself in. The king's pride was hurt. France's Sun King was furious because this party was far superior to any party he had ever given. Nicolas Fouquet had upstaged the king. The famed writer Voltaire later described the situation this way, "At six in the evening, Fouquet was king of France, by two in the morning he was nothing." Indeed, King Louis XIV had Fouquet arrested and sentenced him to life in jail. Then, for good measure, he confiscated the property! Evidently, Louis XIV was very impressed by the Vaux-le-Vicomte estate as it soon served as a model for planning the royal palace in Versailles. The king simply employed the same architects that his minister had used.

Chantilly

COMBINED CASTLE AND MUSEUM

Sitting on an island in the middle of a man-made lake is a chateau steeped in history. Very little is left of the original fortified medieval residence. Each demolition and reconstruction campaign was closely connected to great names in French history, people who lived in Chantilly.

First was Anne de Montmorency. As constable (or chief of the armies) under King François I, in 1515, he fought beside his friend the king, and is credited for the famous military victory at Marignano, Italy. Because Montmorency found the medieval castle too uncomfortable, he made major changes by adding on. But the only part that remains from this period is the "*Petit Chateau*" located to your left when you enter the main courtyard.

The second person was Louis II de Bourbon-Condé, known as "*le Grand Condé*". A contemporary of King Louis XIV, he came from a famous aristocratic family. He commissioned landscape architect André Le Nôtre to design the gardens, fountains and canal. Le Nôtre also designed the gardens in Versailles, Sceaux and Vaux-le-Vicomte.

Lastly, at the end of the 19th century, the Duke of Aumale (one of the sons of King Louis-Philippe) had the "*Grand Chateau*" rebuilt. It was torn down during the French Revolution. This man was an avid collector of art and rare books. Thanks to him, the Chantilly chateau now houses one of the largest museums of master paintings. It is second only to the Louvre museum. Its collections include paintings by Botticelli, Raphaël, Watteau, Delacroix and Ingres.

The prince de Condé

Écouen

A TASTE FOR
THE RENAISSANCE

Anne de Montmorency was incredibly wealthy. He was a friend of both King François I and his successor King Henri II. He not only undertook modernizing the Chantilly chateau, but he also had a new home built for himself and his wife in Écouen, which was constructed over the twenty-year span from 1530 to 1550. Anne de Montmorency had the palace built in the style of his time: Renaissance. The most important change in Renaissance architecture is that instead of a closed fortress, the structure is open to the outside world. Écouen even has a vast terrace framing the landscape. In the medieval ages, moats had a military function. Here, however, they only border three sides of the palace and serve no defensive purpose. The façades are decorated with statues placed in niches. Columns grace the ancient-Greek style porticos. The chateau is now home to the National Museum of Renaissance Art. Its interior decor is authentic Renaissance, and the magnificent painted fireplaces are prime examples of the period. In certain rooms, the ornate friezes (in other words, the painted borders) on the ceiling beams are stunning. You can also see fanciful detailed work called "grotesques."

France's finest set of tapestries is on display in the west wing of the chateau. The group spans 75 meters and relates the Old Testament story about King David's love for Bathsheba.

Constable
Anne de Montmorency

Thoiry

AN ANGLE FOR SUMMER AND WINTER SOLSTICE

Imagine a French chateau with sprawling grounds where giraffes, elephants, antelopes, lions, panthers, tigers, and leopards roam; where hippopotamuses and bears feel at home. Incredible, but true at Thoiry, located a short drive from Paris. The castle sits on the edge of a zoological and botanical park, all part of an African nature reserve. While uncaged exotic animals are the main attraction for visitors, the chateau is actually quite interesting, too.

Raoul Moreau, treasurer to King Henri II, commissioned this palace full of secrets. All its proportions respect the golden rules of architecture. Architects in ancient Greece long ago discovered the formula for calculating length and width to achieve a perfectly harmonious

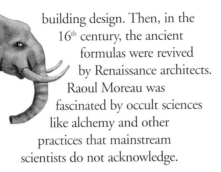

building design. Then, in the 16th century, the ancient formulas were revived by Renaissance architects. Raoul Moreau was fascinated by occult sciences like alchemy and other practices that mainstream scientists do not acknowledge.

Moreau had his hilltop chateau built to be perfectly in line with the sun's rays on the winter solstice (the shortest day of the year, December 21 or 22) and with the sun's rays on the summer solstice (the longest day of the year, June 21 or 22). Year-round, the chateau's central *vestibule*, or entrance hall, is bathed in sun.

Saint-Germain-en-Laye

HOME TO ANCIENT ART

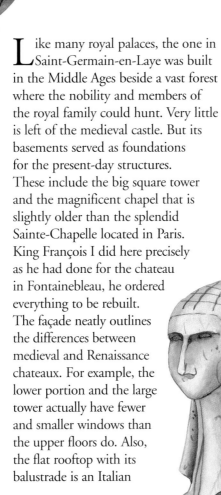

Like many royal palaces, the one in Saint-Germain-en-Laye was built in the Middle Ages beside a vast forest where the nobility and members of the royal family could hunt. Very little is left of the medieval castle. But its basements served as foundations for the present-day structures. These include the big square tower and the magnificent chapel that is slightly older than the splendid Sainte-Chapelle located in Paris. King François I did here precisely as he had done for the chateau in Fontainebleau, he ordered everything to be rebuilt. The façade neatly outlines the differences between medieval and Renaissance chateaux. For example, the lower portion and the large tower actually have fewer and smaller windows than the upper floors do. Also, the flat rooftop with its balustrade is an Italian invention that French architects imported. The Saint-Germain-en-Laye chateau was not only one of French kings' favorite residences, it served as a refuge for royals when there was civil unrest in Paris. King Louis XIV was born in this chateau and spent much of his childhood here, safe from the Fronde (a movement of French nobles in revolt against the absolute monarchy in power). Today, the chateau houses the National Museum of Archeology which features objects dating from prehistoric times to the beginning of the Middle Ages. The estate's terrace offers a magnificent view of Paris.

Vincennes

A ROYAL DONJON

King Charles V

In the Middle Ages, the Vincennes woods (now a Paris park) were still a real forest, teaming with wild game such as deer and boar.

King Philippe Auguste and King Louis IX would often come to hunt, and stayed in what was then just a hunting lodge. In the mid-14th century, King Charles V added on to it, thus creating an imposing fortress surrounded by a protective moat. The watchtowers on the one-kilometer-long outer wall rose up much higher than they do today.

Inside those walls, the most impressive feature was the towering donjon. As at La Roche-Guyon, this was a veritable fortress within a fortress. But quite unlike other fortresses of its time, the donjon at the castle in Vincennes offered comfortable and welcoming furnishings. This was very simply because it was not only the last refuge during a siege, it was also the king's place of residence. Most of the rooms on the six levels of the donjon were spacious, richly decorated and painted. Many pieces of old sculpture give an idea of how luxurious it was, especially the second floor where the royal apartments were located. Charles V was also a great amateur of art and had a sizable library. His manuscript collection contained some absolute gems.

All these treasures were well protected in the donjon, which is still the highest in Europe.

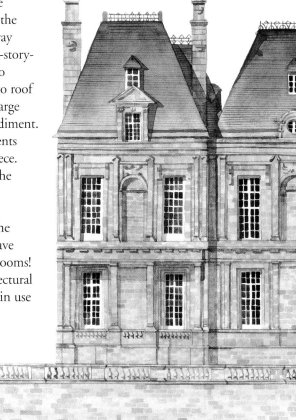

At first, it was just called "Maisons". Then, a rich new owner tacked his name on and it became "Maisons-Laffitte". Rich banker Jacques Laffitte bought this estate in the 1830s. The grounds were parceled up then sold to individuals who wanted to build new homes.

But let's return to the early history of this estate. René de Longueil, Minister of Finance under King Louis XIV, commissioned architect François Mansart to construct a building typical of its time, in a style called "classic revival" as it aimed to achieve harmony and balance in form.

These ideas are expressed by the perfect harmony and symmetry of the façades and the two pavilions on either side of the central unit. The entrance sits exactly in the middle. To make the doorway even more impressive, three-story-high columns were placed to frame it. The columns rise to roof level where they support a large triangle in stone called a pediment. All these architectural elements were created in ancient Greece. Good examples of this are the carved capitals that top the columns.

Typical of Mansart's style, the steep double-sloped roofs gave added, usable space. More rooms! A mansard roof is an architectural term that is still very much in use today all round the world.

Maisons-Laffitte

MANSARD ROOFS AND ATTIC ROOMS

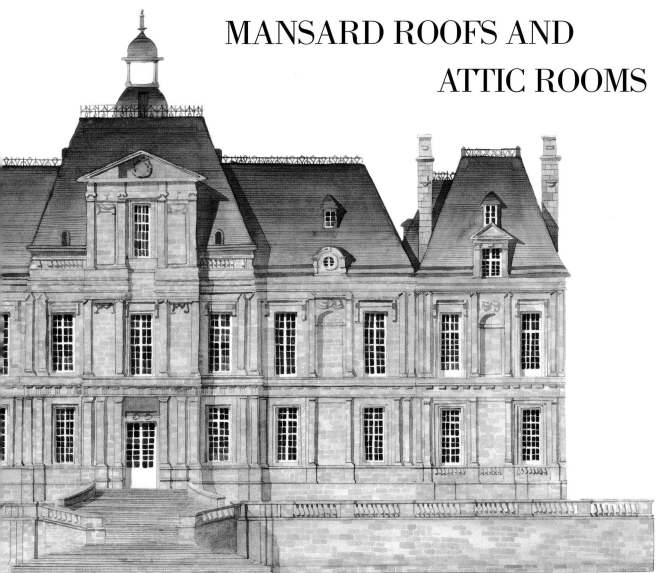

Anet

DIANE'S BED CHAMBER

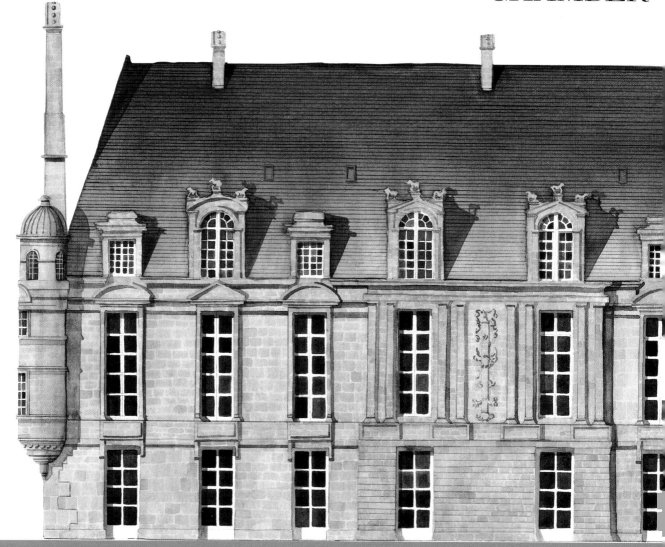

Diana, the goddess of hunting

Philippe Delorme, a quite famous Renaissance-period architect, designed this lovely residence for a very famous lady in French history, Duchess Diane de Poitiers. While she was not the wife of King Henri II, she was close to him and held more influence over the court than did Queen Catherine de Medecis. The main palace gateway is impressive. Its bronze relief representing Diana, the ancient goddess of hunting, is a symbolic way of telling visitors that the chateau belonged to an avid huntress. Diane de Poitiers wanted the hunting theme to be present in all the gateway's sculptured pieces. One of them shows four dogs surrounding a startled deer. Once through the main gateway, visitors enter the old main courtyard.

Little remains of the 16th century Gothic manor and it takes a lot of imagination to picture what it must have looked like. Only one wing of the old palace has survived. Diane's bedroom was on its upper floor. The central portion of the chateau and the opposite wing were torn down during the French Revolution. Fortunately, the chapel survived the Revolution. Today's visitors can admire its splendid, dizzying dome. Its geometric tricks give the impression that everything is being pulled upwards into its spiral. After the death of King Henri II, Catherine de Medecis excluded Diane de Poitiers from the royal court. As so, Diane lived out the rest of her life in her magnificent castle, fit for a king.

Breteuil

ONCE UPON A TIME…

The grounds are beautiful. Breteuil is a castle that has belonged to the same family for centuries. Its architectural style is called "Louis XIII" which is recognizable mainly by the combined use of brick and stone for the façades.

Inside the chateau, several groups of wax mannequins illustrate the history of the Breteuil family. Many of its members played important roles in French government and marked history. In your tour, you may come nose to nose with King Louis XVI and Queen Marie Antoinette or Louis XVIII in his wheelchair. The wax statues in the kitchen show busy servants preparing a lavish meal. The dining room table is already set. In the drawing room, politicians negotiate an important treaty. And so, the chateau's interior gives us a slice of history and an amusing look at daily life long ago. The park also offers a fun tour through some very famous fairy tales. More precisely: the fairy tales written by Charles Perrault. Sleeping Beauty slumbers as Prince Charming and her Fairy Godmother stand by her side. Over there, Little Red Riding Hood is off to visit her grandmother. And, look! There goes Puss in Boots!

The baron de Breteuil

Dampierre

REFINED CASTLE LIFE

Back in the days of King Louis XIV, the duc de Chevreuse (son-in-law of the king's powerful minister Colbert) had this palace built on the site of an old castle. In the courtyard, two turrets from the original castle have survived. The royal palace in Versailles served as inspiration. Dampierre had to be smaller, of course, as nobody was supposed to be as wealthy as the king. In fact, the construction was overseen by two of the Versailles palace architects, Jules Hardouin-Mansart and André Le Nôtre. Mansart was in charge of architecture while Le Nôtre designed the formal gardens, man-made lake, canals, fountains and cascades.

Living the life of luxury required more than just living in a palace, it required making the palace live. It needed numerous servants and expensive carriages. The architecture at Dampierre gives a fine example of this combination. The main hall of the palace is ringed by moats filled with water and flanked by outbuildings used as stables, garages, kitchens and domestics' living quarters. The palace's impressive ballroom, called *"salle Minerve"*, was named after the Roman goddess of wisdom, Minerva.

In the 19th century, the great artist Ingres began a vast mural. Unfortunately, he died before he could finish it.

The duc de Chevreuse

Compiègne

FROM CHARLEMAGNE TO NAPOLEON

The history of the successive castles at Compiègne is tightly interwoven with the history of the French monarchy. The first royal residence in this city was actually built before the Carolingian period, the dynasty of Emperor Charlemagne. The hunting-lodge aspect and forest location of this chateau made it very popular with numerous kings. Of all the royal palaces in the Paris area, Compiègne was a favorite, right up there on list beside Versailles and Fontainebleau. From the 15th century onwards, newly crowned kings would have a nice long

stay in Compiègne after their coronation celebration in the cathedral in Reims. In the Middle Ages, King Charles V had the castle rebuilt. Then, much later, King Louis XIV had apartments added because he found the place terribly uncomfortable. He quipped, "In Versailles, I am lodged like a king; in Fontainebleau, like a prince; in Compiègne, like a peasant."

It is hard for us today to know how true that was, because it was all torn down. The chateau that we can visit today was built for Louis XV. Overseeing the construction was Ange-Jacques Gabriel, one of the best-known architects at that time. Taking his inspiration from Antiquity, Gabriel gave his buildings austere classic-revival architectural elements like the high columns and pediments on the façades. Napoleon I, then Napoleon III, greatly enjoyed their stays in Compiègne. Their sumptuous and luxuriously decorated apartments are now open to the general public.

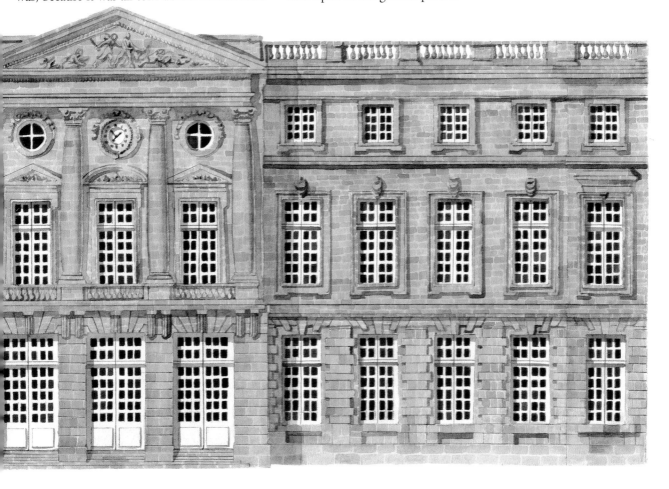

Ferrières

LET THE SUNSHINE IN!

What wiser decision could a wealthy art collector take than to build his own palace to display his collection of fine art? This is precisely what Baron James de Rothschild did in the mid-19th century. His mansion sits in the center of magnificent, landscaped grounds. Its history does not go back to the Middle Ages, the Renaissance or even to the classic revival style. It was new! But Joseph Paxton, a famous English architect, did incorporate styles from the past.

The exterior gives us four very different façades. Each one is unique. As with the interior design, they play off on various elements from the French and the Italian Renaissance. The most prestigious room is the two-story-high main hall. While the Baron's tapestries and paintings were moved out long ago, the neo-Renaissance architecture still dazzles visitors.

Tall columns support the upper gallery circling the room. Twelve meters up, a large skylight lets sunlight flood the hall. Lighting a room with roof-level windows was a technological exploit in the 19th century as it required using iron - then, a totally new building material in architecture. But Paxton had already gained considerable experience with iron by building London's famous Crystal Palace and several greenhouses.

The baron de Rothschild

Rambouillet

The chateau in Rambouillet dates back to the Middle Ages when an advisor to King Charles V had a fortified royal residence built here. The only remaining part of it is the big tower on the other side of the façades depicted in the drawing. The castle underwent several renovations. The present-day façades were completed about a century and a half ago.

This chateau has been marked by history. King François I died here. For over a century, it has served as a presidential palace. Presidents frequently lodge their high-ranking guests here. Most are statesmen on official visits. Conferences and summits are also held here. It is nevertheless open to the public provided, of course, neither the president nor any guest is present. Visitors can admire richly decorated rooms with splendid furnishings.

Water is a major feature in and around this beautiful park. Louis XVI had a dairy farm built here to amuse his wife, Marie Antoinette. He hoped that this might reconcile her with the chateau that queen detested and had nicknamed "the toad house" (la crapaudière). A man-made cave closes the two rooms where they enjoyed sipping fresh milk. Water gurgles in a fountain. Overlooking it all is a statue of a nymph – a Greek goddess – and her goat.

WHERE PRESIDENTS MEET

Champs-sur-Marne

A FAMILY HOME

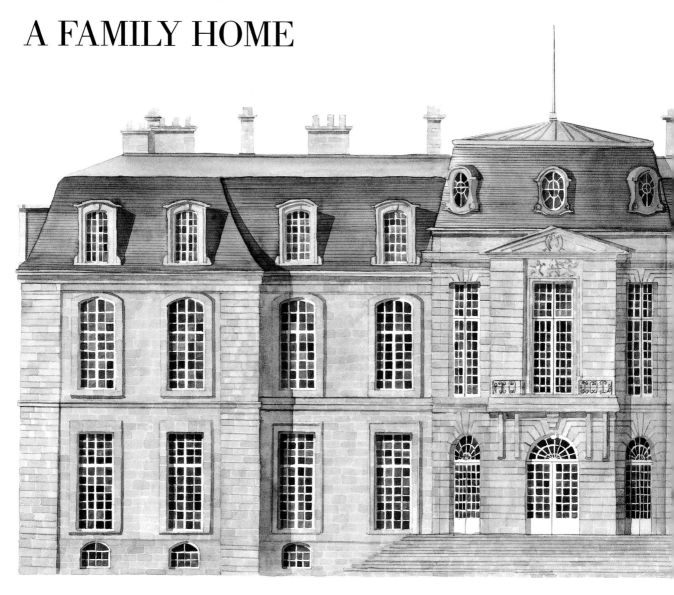

This small charming palace is located in the middle of one of the most beautiful parks of Ile-de-France (the greater Paris area). The nephew and disciple of the great landscape architect André Le Nôtre laid out the park. At the end of the reign of Louis XIV, a rich financier named Paul Poisson de Bourvalais decided to construct a palace on the land. Unfortunately for him, a few years later he lost all his money. Maintaining such a grand home costs a lot, and he could no longer afford it. Thereafter, the estate changed hands several times. Among the numerous owners were the dukes of La Vallière who enjoyed inviting great thinkers like Diderot, d'Alembert and Voltaire to come and stay. This was the Age of Enlightenment, full of new and

The marquise de Pompadour

luminous ideas. The palace was also rented out to wealthy noblemen. The Marquise de Pompadour, King Louis XV's mistress, lived at Champs-sur-Marne for several years. But this palace is interesting for other reasons. It shows us how the concepts of interior comforts have changed over time. Unlike the chateaux of previous periods, Versailles included, this palace was designed with hallways! It was a new concept. It made a huge difference for privacy. Now each room became independent; no more cutting through one room to get to another. Another major improvement was a private bathroom or toilet for each apartment in the palace, thus giving occupants privacy. Then came the novel idea of having one large room reserved for meals and located off the living room. Before this, meals had always been served by setting up a table in an antechamber.

Not too far from the Fontainebleau forest is Courances, a site that has been shaped and reshaped through the centuries. Each generation of owners modernized and restyled the home. The unimposing 16th-century mansion was demolished in the following century to make way for the H-shaped and much more comfortable chateau that we see today. The following generations modified the main courtyard and other portions. They opened up new windows. They removed older decorative pieces from the façades. When Baron Samuel de Haber bought the chateau in the second half of the 19th century, he decided that rather than updating the style, he would restore the palace to its original Louis XIII style, putting the accent on the mix of red brick and gray stone. But Hippolyte Destailleur, the baron's architect, went over and beyond the neo-Louis XIII style. He also let his imagination run wild and created high chimneys, changed the roof lines and added grandiose outdoor staircases leading to the gardens. Inspiration came from the nearby chateau in Fontainebleau.

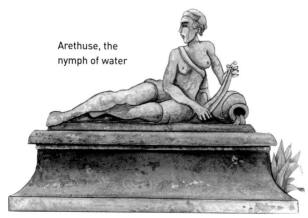

Arethuse, the nymph of water

Courances

BRICK AND STONE

Provins

THE CAESAR TOWER

A lord of the
Middle Ages

Legend mistakenly has it that Roman emperor Julius Caesar founded the city of Provins and built the great tower. In fact, it was not until the Middle Ages that the tower was commissioned by Henry I "The Liberal", Count of Champagne. Back in the 12th century, the town of Provins played a major part in trade. Twice a year, its fairs drew merchants from all over Europe. Still today, the upper city and the lower city offer plenty of medieval vestiges for attentive strollers. There are ramparts, houses, churches, and of course, the famous Caesar Tower. Built on the hilltop overlooking the town, the watchtower served several purposes. Like the towers at La Roche-Guyon and Vincennes, it offered the count and his soldiers a place of refuge in case of danger. The count's palace, hardly recognizable today, was located nearby. Given its height, it was an ideal watchtower. Approaching enemies would not go unnoticed! The donjon was also used as prison. Its thick, impressive fortress walls could not be easily scaled. The tower symbolized the power that the counts of Champagne wielded over the local nobility who had to submit to the counts' authority with "fidelity and homage".

Art work: Isabelle Chemin
Layout: Marylène Lhenri
Editing: Laurence Solnais
Aknowledgements to Marcelle Guerrot

Photoengraving: Alésia Studio, Paris
Printed by Escourbiac Graulhet

Printed March 2006

Legal Deposit Avril 2006

ISBN 10 : 2-84096-462-7

ISBN 13 : 978-2-84096-462-9

Respects French Law no. 49-965 on publications for young readers